London Bridge is Falling Down

Distributed by The Child's World®
1980 Lookout Drive • Mankato, MN 56003-1705
800-599-READ • www.childsworld.com

Acknowledgments
The Child's World®: Mary Berendes, Publishing Director
The Design Lab: Kathleen Petelinsek, Design

Library of Congress Cataloging-in-Publication Data
Austin, Michael, 1965-
London Bridge is falling down / illustrated by Michael Allen Austin.
    p. cm.
ISBN 978-1-60954-292-4 (library bound: alk. paper)
1. Folk songs, English—England—Texts. [1. Folk songs—England.
2. Singing games. 3. Games.] I. Title.
PZ8.3.A9372Lo 2011
782.42—dc22
[E]   2010032428

Printed in the United States of America in Mankato, Minnesota.
December 2010
PA02074

ILLUSTRATED BY MICHAEL ALLEN AUSTIN

London Bridge is falling down,
falling down, falling down.
London Bridge is falling down,
my fair lady.

Build it up with wood and clay,
wood and clay, wood and clay.
Build it up with wood and clay,
my fair lady.

Wood and clay will wash away,
wash away, wash away.
Wood and clay will wash away,
my fair lady.

Build it up with iron and steel,
iron and steel, iron and steel.
Build it up with iron and steel,
my fair lady.

Iron and steel will bend and bow,
bend and bow, bend and bow.
Iron and steel will bend and bow,
my fair lady.

Build it up with silver and gold,
silver and gold, silver and gold.
Build it up with silver and gold,
my fair lady.

Silver and gold will be stolen away,
stolen away, stolen away.
Silver and gold will be stolen away,
my fair lady.

SONG ACTIVITY

London Bridge is falling down,
falling down, falling down.
London Bridge is falling down,
my fair lady.

Build it up with wood and clay,
wood and clay, wood and clay.
Build it up with wood and clay,
my fair lady.

Wood and clay will wash away,
wash away, wash away.
Wood and clay will wash away,
my fair lady.

Build it up with iron and steel,
iron and steel, iron and steel.
Build it up with iron and steel,
my fair lady.

Iron and steel will bend and bow,
bend and bow, bend and bow.
Iron and steel will bend and bow,
my fair lady.

Build it up with silver and gold,
silver and gold, silver and gold.
Build it up with silver and gold,
my fair lady.

Silver and gold will be stolen away,
stolen away, stolen away.
Silver and gold will be stolen away,
my fair lady.

Two players face each other and join their hands above their heads to make an arch. While singing the song, other players walk under the arch. When the song reaches the word "lady," the two arch players lower their joined arms and "capture" the player underneath.

BENEFITS OF NURSERY RHYMES AND ACTIVITY SONGS

Activity songs and nursery rhymes are more than just a fun way to pass the time. They are a rich source of intellectual, emotional, and physical development for a young child. Here are some of their benefits:

❀ Learning the words and activities builds the child's self-confidence—"I can do it all by myself!"

❀ The repetitious movements build coordination and motor skills.

❀ The close physical interaction between adult and child reinforces both physical and emotional bonding.

❀ In a context of "fun," the child learns the art of listening in order to learn.

❀ Learning the words expands the child's vocabulary. He or she learns the names of objects and actions that are both familiar and new.

❀ Repeating the words helps develop the child's memory.

❀ Learning the words is an important step toward learning to read.

❀ Reciting the words gives the child a grasp of English grammar and how it works. This enhances the development of language skills.

❀ The rhythms and rhyming patterns sharpen listening skills and teach the child how poetry works. Eventually the child learns to put together his or her own simple rhyming words— "I made a poem!"

ABOUT THE ILLUSTRATOR

Michael Allen Austin learned what it might be like on London Bridge when an underground spring was found flowing under his studio. Now, when he paints, he keeps one eye watching for leaks. He lives in Atlanta with his wife and sheepdog, who often show up in his books.